Notes / Ex

Welcome to IONA

with text and pictures by JOHN BROOKS

This book is dedicated to those who have made the journey to this tiny, beautiful island; often coming from distant countries, other continents, to see Iona and pay homage to the great saint that once lived here. In Dr Johnson's words:

'We were now treading that illustrious Island, which was once the luminary of the Caledonian regions, whence savage clans and roving barbarians derived the benefits of knowledge, and the blessings of religion. To abstract the mind from all local emotion would be impossible, if it were endeavoured, and would be foolish if it were possible. Whatever withdraws us from the power of our senses, whatever makes the past, the distant, or the future, predominate over the present, advances us in the dignity of thinking beings. Far from me, and from my friends, be such frigid philosophy as may conduct us indifferent and unmoved over any ground which has been dignified by wisdom, bravery, or virture. That man is little to be envied, whose patriotism would not gain force upon the plain of Marathon, or whose piety would not grow warmer among the ruins of *Iona*.'

BELOW: *This plaque is to be found in a wall on the way to the Abbey from the Village, and contains the latter part of the above quotation.*

Centuries before the arrival of St Columba on Iona in 563 the island had been adopted as a centre of religion by sun-worshipping Druids. Like Columba, these priests of the Dark Ages must have sensed something unique in the atmosphere of Iona, a quality that still sets it apart as a spiritual oasis. Perhaps it is the sparkling clarity of its light that appealed to these early mystics, for here the sky seems to open directly to Heaven not only as the sun goes down in incomparable splendour, but throughout any sunny day when the cloud that hangs over the mainland and Mull miraculously breaks to bathe Iona in light that seems even brighter against the sombre unlit hills on the opposite shore. Of course it's no use pretending that Iona escapes those days of unrelieved wetness that Western Scotland produces quite regularly, but it is true that Iona

enjoys a substantial amount more sunshine than places to the east. Thus on the day that the photograph above was taken Craignure suffered cloud and rain while barely a drop fell here.

Iona is a tiny island – only three and a half miles long by one and a half broad – separated from Mull by about a mile of usually choppy water. Winter gales can sometimes cut the island off for days. Regular visitors to Iona travel through Mull by car or coach and cross the Sound of Iona by ferry from Fionnphort. Many other people come by steamer from Oban and are ferried ashore by small boats. Both ways the landing-point is the same: the quay just to the south of the Cathedral, at the foot of the street lined with cottages that is the main thoroughfare of the village. There are only about seventy houses on the island, and about twenty of them are here, on The Street. This climbs up quite steeply to meet another lane coming from the middle of the island. At this junction there is a lovely ruin on the right, the remains of the Benedictine Nunnery founded in 1203 by Reginald Macdonald of Islay, Lord of the Isles. Visitors to the Cathedral turn right here, while those who have time to explore more of the island could take the other turning that leads to the south of the island and Port a' Churaich, the Port of the Coracle, where Columba first set foot on the island.

Columba was a man of some importance even before he began his self-imposed exile on Iona. He came of royal Irish blood and could well have been King of Ireland had he not made the Church his vocation. His birth was foretold by St Patrick and by his disciple, Maucta, and an angel came to his mother in a dream on the night before his birth to tell of 'one who would be reckoned as one of the prophets of God who should lead innumerable souls to the heavenly country'. As far as we know Columba was born on 7 December 521 near Lough Gartan in Donegal. At this time Ireland was famous for its learning and Columba enjoyed as fine an education as was

BELOW: *The ferry from Fionnphort brings another party of visitors to Iona's quay on St Ronan's Bay. Just to the south is Martyr's Bay where sixty-eight monks were slain by Norse invaders in 806 and where the bodies of the Chiefs and Kings were disembarked before burial in the Reilig Oran.*

possible in those early times, attending a monastic school at Moville, not far from Belfast, and being attached to a succession of wise men of the Church as a pupil, for from the first it was decided that he should be dedicated to that career. Finally, he went to Clonard to study with the famous St Finnian, who attracted many of the brightest intellects of Europe to the small town, and here Columba spent much time reading and copying the rare manuscripts of the community. At this time Ireland was 'glittering with saints who were as numerous as the stars of Heaven', so that it was natural that there should be eleven outstanding young men of the Church at Clonard with Columba: these 'Twelve Apostles of Ireland' were all canonised, and later Columba chose eleven disciples to accompany him to set up his community on Iona. His early

manhood, from the time he was twenty-five until he was forty, was taken up with travelling about Ireland, teaching and setting up monasteries and churches (he is said to have founded thirty-seven monasteries in Ireland alone). Amongst them was the one at Kells, famous for the illuminated copy of the Gospels now in Trinity College, Dublin. The community on Iona were forced to flee here after Columba's death because of the raids of the Vikings.

However, the way of life was hardly peaceful in Ireland even then, with the

numerous chieftains constantly fighting amongst themselves (and easing their consciences by giving a proportion of their plunder to the monasteries). Inevitably Columba became involved in one of these feuds when one of the local princes violated the sanctity of his church, pursuing and capturing a noble fugitive who was then killed. Columba sought the support of his powerful family and took his clans to battle led, it is said, by the Archangel Michael himself. Columba won a magnificent triumph, losing only one man (and that because he broke a sacred taboo) and slaying three thousand of the enemy, who were pagans. He

attributed the victory to the power of
Christianity. Yet Columba's success
brought him trouble for many of the
saints and elders of the Irish church were
jealous of him and in his absence ex-
communicated him for causing the need-
less deaths of three thousand men. Later
the excommunication was rescinded and

instead Columba was told to go out and win as many souls for the Church as had been lost in the battle.

Although he felt that he had been unjustly treated by the Synod, Columba felt remorse for the slaughter he had caused and spent some time in travelling about Ireland from one holy man to another seeking advice as to what he should do. Before the battle, Archangel Michael had spoken to him in a dream, answering his prayers for victory by granting him success with the proviso that afterwards, to regain God's Grace, he should exile himself from his beloved Ireland and the spiritual stimulus of his fellow saints. Thus there was only one course of action open to Columba – he had to undertake a pilgrimage to a place out of sight of Ireland, and so, selecting twelve followers (mainly from his own family) he set sail from his native land in the early summer of 563, heading northwards to the islands off the coast of western Scotland.

The coracle in which the twelve sailed was a frail craft with a framework of slender, pliable branches covered by hides made taut by leather thongs laced to the top edge of the frame. As the new hides were allowed to dry after an initial soaking they moulded themselves to the contour of the boat, and made a reasonably buoyant sea-going craft which could stand up to the battering of the rough seas of the Hebrides. Although it was a much larger boat than the one-man coracles of South Wales that are still used today, the broad principles of construction were similar, and one can only wonder at the courage and strong constitutions of

the men who undertook such long voyages in such fragile vessels.

On his way northwards Columba called at the Irish colony on Kintyre whose chief was a kinsman, grandson of the founder of this Christian settlement, Fergus Mor, who had left Ireland for Argyll some seventy years before. They only rested a few days here, however, before hurrying on to Oronsay, a tiny island separated from the larger Colonsay by a tidal causeway. From its highest point Ireland was still visible, so Columba and his twelve followers again boarded the coracle and continued their voyage, landing at last in a tiny cove on the south coast of the island, subsequently known as Port a'Churaich, Port of the Coracle.

Their first sight of the island could hardly have been encouraging, for this side of Iona presents an inhospitable face to the sea, the little bay where they landed being flanked by steep cliffs, with a cluster of rocky islets (skerries) just offshore. Nor, when the party climbed up from the bay, was the landscape that met their eyes any more welcoming. The southern end of the island is barren, a rocky wasteland that may appeal to visitors escaping from all the cares of the modern world to 'get away from it all', but was hardly encouraging to the group of men who had come here to found a self-supporting community dedicated to the life of the spirit. Columba quickly spotted a small hill that looked to the south-west, and on reaching its summit searched the horizon for the shape of the Irish coast; it could not be seen and ever since the hill has been called Carn-Cul-ri-Eirinn, the hill with its back to Ireland. In spite of the discouraging scene before them, Columba and his followers decided to explore the island and set off northwards. Soon the rocks and heather gave way to the grass of the machair, the pastureland unique to the Hebrides and

LEFT: *The beautiful decoration of St Martin's Cross, in front of the West Door of the Cathedral. This is its eastern face; on the other side there are scenes from the Old Testament and a cameo of the Virgin and Child. It dates from the ninth century.*

scattered parts of the coast of western Scotland where shell-sand gives the shallow soil doses of much-needed lime. Exploring further to the east they found better land still, for the machair, for all its richness, has little shelter from the force of westerly gales, but the north-eastern section of the island has rich pastures protected by the hills that culminate in Dun I, which at 332 feet is the principal summit of Iona.

Whether there was anyone on the island to greet Columba and his followers is open to conjecture; there is a pleasing mixture of folk-tales and untrustworthy documentary evidence on the point. One legend has it that there was already a community here when Columba landed but that the saint, sensing that the leaders were bogus, told them to leave and they at once bowed to his authority. Many

writers tell of Iona being sacred to the Druids and a burial-place of their kings. One twentieth-century author (Neil M. Gunn: *Off in a Boat*) mentions 360 sculptured stones on the island as being pre-Christian, which would make Iona rival Callanish on Lewis as the Stonehenge of Scotland. He also speaks of three white marble stones that rested in hollows on a great slab which each visitor to the island would turn three times sunwise, thus perpetuating a Druidical rite. Then, too, there were the Black Stones of Iona on which the early Kings of the Isles took their oaths: should anyone perjure themselves when taking an oath on the stones then he would turn black.

The last of these vanished about a hundred years ago and legend has it that the Coronation Stone in Westminster Abbey is one of the Black Stones.

The saint is also featured in many legends. A macabre one relates how, when first landing on the island, one of his followers, St Oran, suggests that he is buried alive as a living sacrifice to the island which will thus be sanctified. Columba accepts this offer and so Oran is buried. After three days Columba and his followers opened up the grave and were horrified to find Oran still alive, and as he spoke the words, 'There is no such great wonder in death, nor is hell what it has been described', Columba hastily ordered, 'Earth, earth on Oran's eyes, lest he further blab', and so the unfortunate Oran was re-entombed. This story too has a Druidical flavour to it, and seems out of character even to a warrior-saint!

Returning to Columba's arrival on the island, he and his followers were soon busy establishing their church. It was situated just to the north of the Cathedral, and no traces of the original settlement remain except rough foundations of stone on the little hillock opposite the west door of the Cathedral, Torr Abb. These were the remains of his cell where he slept on the bare rock. The outer

BELOW: *Iona Abbey and Cathedral; Torr Abb (Columba's Cell) is the hillock on the left, and beyond the Cathedral, in the Sound of Iona, is Eilean nam Ban, the Isle of the Women, where the laymen of the monastic community kept their wives.*

covering of the beehive-shaped building was a wooden framework which supported a roof of turf. The other buildings of the earliest abbey followed the same pattern, though the church itself would have been rectangular.

Columba's saintliness and his power of leadership soon attracted more followers, and so his church grew. More buildings were added to the monastery and more fields tilled to support the expanding community. Iona was an oasis of Christian culture in a largely hostile pagan world, and soon Columba was able to send out his monks to the pagan tribes to attempt to convert them to Christianity; later the saintly abbot undertook voyages of conversion himself. Often he turned away hostility by performing miracles, once saving one of his monks from the wrath of the Loch Ness monster itself. The legend relates that Columba, about to cross the River Ness, came across men burying the body of a colleague who had just been killed by a monster. The ferry was on the other side of the river and one of the monks fearlessly began to swim across the river so that he could bring it to the bank where his abbot and the rest of the party waited. The monster, seeing more easy prey, rushed towards the poor monk with a fearsome roar, its mouth wide open. As it was about to swallow the man in one gulp Columba raised his hand and made the Sign of the Cross commanding the

monster to leave the monk alone, where-upon it turned round and rushed away leaving the heathens on the bank amazed at the power of Columba's God.

Columba also expanded the power of his church by means of political manœuvring and diplomacy (the former usually being justified by dreams given by God to the saint to guide his actions). Thus by conversion of heathen kings, and by support of Christian princes against pagan heirs apparent, Columba's in-fluence spread across Scotland. He is said to have founded more than a hundred churches 'which the wave frequents', and his friend St Cainnech (who gave his name to the island of Inch Kenneth, close to Iona off the west coast of Mull)

ABOVE: *The monument to George Douglas Campbell, eighth Duke of Argyll, and his wife which is in the South Transept of the Cathedral. He gave the Abbey to the Church of Scotland in 1899, who promised that all denominations could use it.*

founded churches far away on the coast of Fife. It is startling to remember that it was only in the year before the death of Columba (596) that Pope Gregory the Great, seeing English slaves in the streets of Rome, sent Augustine on a voyage of conversion to the land of the Angles. By then Columba was venerated as one of the greatest of holy men, and Iona attracted visitors from all over Europe who wished to pay their respects to him.

Approaching the Abbey from the Village the visitor first comes to the Reilig Oran, or Oran's graveyard, better known as the burial-place of the Kings. Like the Abbey, this lies on the right of the road, looking out to a marvellous panorama of the hills of Mull and the Sound of Iona. St Oran was one of Columba's disciples and in the grounds of the Chapel dedicated to him are the tombs of sixty kings, forty-eight of them Scottish, four Irish, and eight Norwegian. Duncan and his murderer, Macbeth, lie here on

> *. . . Colme-kill,*
> *The sacred storehouse of his* [Duncan's]
>   *predecessors*
> *And guardian of their bones.*
> (Macbeth Act II, Scene 4)

(In the Gaelic tongue the island is called I Chaluim-Chille.) The last kings to be buried here were interred in the eleventh century, before the Conqueror invaded England. No trace of the tombs remain now: the collection of tombstones in the enclosures date from late medieval times. St Oran's Chapel has its own humble beauty and was probably built in the ninth or tenth century, though the Norman archway of the door is, of course, a later addition.

Close to the west door of the Abbey a cobbled street has been uncovered which is the last section of the Sraid nam Marbh (the Street of the Dead). It provided a paved way from Martyr's Bay (where one can still see the mound [the Ealadh] where the bier rested after being brought ashore to the door of the Abbey itself. This was the route used by the funeral processions of the Chiefs and Kings on their way to the Reilig Oran. Outside the west door of the Abbey stand two great crosses. The first, dating from the ninth century, is that of St Martin; it has slots in its arms to hold wooden extensions, while the centre of its west face bears a cameo of the Virgin and Child. Old Testament scenes decorate this side of the granite shaft, while the east side has abstract ornamental carving. At the base is a weathered inscription which reads, 'A prayer for the servant of Christ who made this cross'. The other cross is dedicated to St John and is a moulded copy of the original which suffered from being blown down so frequently by gales sweeping the island. Originally it had marble bosses set into the granite of its arms and shaft.

Entering the Abbey by the west door the view that meets our eyes is the one shown in the illustration on the opposite page. The nave was the part of the church reserved for the lay people: the ordained inmates of the monastery occupied the choir (which did not extend so far to the east as it does today). Although only fragments remain of the Abbey founded by Reginald Macdonald of Islay early in the thirteenth century, later additions and restorations have been harmonious even though they have been spread over many centuries. The greater part of the fabric dates from *c.* 1420 when the Abbey had to be rebuilt after fifty years of neglect under the abbacy of Fingon Mackinnon. The tower and the choir were completely remodelled at this time. Moving down the nave we see the remains of stone coffins cemented into the floor. They were placed there when the building was restored by the eighth Duke of Argyll in 1899. It is his tomb, with that of his wife, that occupies the south transept. The oak screen that separates the opposing transept from the crossing was the gift of H.M. the Queen in 1956. Note the beautiful painting of the crucified Christ by Roy le Maistre that hangs here. The choir (east

RIGHT: *The nave of St Mary's Cathedral, from the West Door.*

end of the church) contains beautiful medieval carvings on the capitals of the arches of the south aisle. The beautiful Sacristy doorway in the north aisle, with its trefoil arch, dates from the fifteenth century and has been moved here from elsewhere. Beside it is an effigy of Abbot John Mackinnon who died *c.* 1499 and was the last Abbot of Iona. He wears a mitre, a privilege granted to the abbots of Iona by Pope Innocent IV in 1247. The Communion table is made of Iona marble from a quarry in the south of the island.

It is unusual for an abbey church to have its cloisters situated on its north side, but reasons of drainage dictated this site here. On the west side there are remains of two medieval arches, but basically the rest of the Abbey buildings are modern, dating from the foundation of the Iona Community in 1938 (though, of course, only the secular parts date from then, the Duke of Argyll's restoration of the Cathedral having been completed in 1910). Material help in restoring the Abbey so that it could be used by the Community came from all over the world. Thus the timber in the refectory was given by Norway, and the Michael

ABOVE: *The bronze plaque close to the church (on the way to the Cathedral from the Village) explains the origin of the parish church, which now serves a community of about a hundred.*
LEFT: *Maclean's Cross is exquisitely decorated and dates from the fifteenth century.*

Chapel was restored through the generosity of South Africans. The Museum, containing more interesting gravestones, was helped by the Carnegie Trust.

The death of Columba before the altar of the Abbey on 9 June 597 marked the zenith of the monastic community on Iona. However, its influence was to continue for some considerable time yet; missionary Columbans travelled to remote communities preaching Christianity, even reaching the far south of England. The Columban (Celtic) Church had split from the Church of Rome over details such as the correct date for the celebration of Easter, and this autonomy was to continue for some centuries, such was its power. The most important outpost of the Columbans was established at Lindisfarne, Holy Island, off the coast of Northumberland, where they made a second Iona. The monks here shared their

ABOVE: *Continue northwards on the lane running past the Abbey and a succession of delightful scenes will meet the eye, like this typically Hebridean landscape. From the north end of the island the distinctive shape of Staffa and other outlying islands can be clearly seen. There are great expanses of dazzling shell sand that lead down to the sea's edge which has a clarity of colour unmatched elsewhere. Just to the west is Iona's greatest eminence, Dun I, which is 332 feet above sea level and worth the climb for the wonderful panorama of sea and islands from the summit. It is said that good luck follows those that make the ascent seven times.*

founder's enthusiasm for calligraphy, producing such masterpieces as the Lindisfarne Gospels now in the British Museum.

A century after the death of Columba it was felt that a shrine of gold and silver should be made to contain the remains of Columba, and thus present a fitting setting for the sacred relics that pilgrims flocked to Iona to see and pray before. The pilgrims brought yet more prosperity to the Abbey, and unfortunately this attracted the unwelcome attention of Scandinavian pirates that were becoming the scourge of these western seas. The first of the Viking attacks took place in 794 when much damage was done to the monastic buildings. Seven years later the Abbey was gutted by the Norsemen, and in 806 the event was repeated yet more savagely

with the slaying of sixty-eight monks on the beach close to the present jetty; this is now known as Martyrs' Bay. After this disaster the shrine of Columba was moved to Kells in Ireland, though a handful of brave monks remained on Iona to guard the other holy relics. Unwisely, perhaps, the next abbot brought back the shrine from Ireland. In 825 Norsemen again landed on the island and when the abbot refused to tell them the whereabouts of the Abbey's shrine and treasure they killed him and the faithful monks who remained there with him. The two stone coffins in the nave of the Cathedral are said to be those of this abbot (Blaithmac) and Columba.

After this there was a long period of peace until in 986 Vikings from the Norse colony on Dublin Bay plundered the island and killed the abbot and fifteen monks on the dazzling sands at the northern tip of Iona, subsequently known as the White Strand of the Monks. This was the end of Viking invasions; the next historical event of importance was the visit of King Malcolm Canmore and his English Queen, Margaret. It was her forceful arguments that turned many supporters of the Celtic church to that of Rome, and she may have restored the Abbey as well as 'the smaller church of Columcille' (St Oran's Chapel). A handful of Columban monks remained until 1203 when the Abbey was again rebuilt, this time by Reginald MacDonald of Islay, Lord of the Isles, as a Benedictine monastery.

Only part of the charm of Iona lies in the richness of her associations with the early Christian Church in Britain. The great beauty of their surroundings must have aided the spiritual lives of those who lived on the island with Columba and subsequently. Adamnan, the saint's biographer, frequently stresses the inspiration that Columba drew from natural

BELOW: *Port Ban is a sheltered cove on the west side of the island facing the Atlantic. To the south is the wide 'Bay at the Back of the Ocean' and the famous Spouting Cave, where the force of the waves sends a plume of water over a hundred feet into the air in rough weather.*

beauty. With the re-establishment of a religious community on the island perhaps Columba's famous prophecy is fulfilled:

> *Iona of my heart,*
> *Iona of my love,*
> *Instead of monks' voices*
> *Shall be the lowing of cattle;*
> *But ere the world come to an end,*
> *Iona shall be as it was.*

Today this island offers us the rare chance of escaping from nearly all of the unwelcome trappings of the twentieth century; to a great many people it is the desert island of dreams come true – whether or not one is religious there is a spiritual peace to be found here, perhaps best reflected in the words of the composer Mendelssohn, after his visit to Iona in 1829:

'. . . when in some future time I shall sit in a madly crowded assembly with music and dancing round me, and the wish arises to retire into the loneliest loneliness, I shall think of Iona. . . .'

BELOW: *Port of the Coracle, where St Columba first set foot on Iona, is at the southern end of the island. It is remarkable for the myriad hues of the pebbles thrown up and polished by the rough seas that climb up the steep beach. The high ridge at the back of the beach is supposed to be where Columba's followers buried his coracle.*

LEFT: *The Duke's Cross stands by the road to the northern tip of Iona as a memorial to the wife of the eighth Duke of Argyll and was erected in 1879.*

ABOVE: *It is said that a favourite excursion of St Columba during his last years was to the tiny Hill of the Seat that overlooks this, the Beach of the Seat. It is at the northern end of the island and offers the tranquillity that is the hallmark of the island.*

BELOW: *Two old engravings from the Duke of Argyll's book on Iona (published in 1871) show* (TOP) *the view towards Mull from the Reilig Oran and* (BOTTOM) *the view from the north end of the island, with Staffa on the right.*
OPPOSITE: *Another engraving, from the same source, of the Cathedral in ruins at that date.*